Acknowledgements

Illustrations by Tessa Richardson-Jones
Photographs by Zul Mukhida except for: p. 8t Paul Harmer;
pp. 10, 14 National Resource Sensing Centre Ltd;
p. 26 E. T. Archive; p. 27 Nasa, Goddard Institute for
Space Studies/Science Photo Library.

The author and publisher would like to thank the staff and
pupils of Balfour Infant School, Brighton,
Lynette Rowbottom, NRSC and Jane Salazar.

A CIP catalogue record for this book is available
from the British Library.

ISBN 0-7136-4153-3

First published 1995 by A & C Black (Publishers) Ltd
35 Bedford Row, London WC1R 4JH

© 1995 A & C Black (Publishers) Ltd

Typeset in 13/20pt Univers Medium by
Rowland Phototypesetting Ltd, Bury St Edmunds, Suffolk
Printed and bound in the U.K. by
Hunter and Foulis Limited, Edinburgh

going places

Finding the way

Barbara Taylor

Illustrations by Tessa Richardson-Jones
Photographs by Zul Mukhida

Contents

A & C Black · London

What is a map?

A map is a flat drawing of an area on the ground, showing what it looks like from above. It can help you to find places and to work out how far away they are. Maps can also show the best way of getting to a place.

Have you ever used a map?

I used a globe to find out where Gran went on holiday.

This road atlas showed me the quickest route to Auntie Jean's.

I took this map with me on a sponsored walk.

Maps can be different shapes and sizes and show large or small areas. Maps showing large areas, such as maps of the world, can help you to find places hundreds of kilometres away in other countries.

Maps of small areas can show places in more detail, pointing out features such as roads, forests, lakes and buildings.

Look carefully at these three maps. Which map would you use to:

a) Find out where the buried treasure is?
b) Find your way around a new town?
c) Find your pen friend's home town?

(The answers are at the bottom of the page.)

Answers:

Map 1 = b   Map 2 = c   Map 3 = a

Looking from above

Have you ever looked down at the ground from the top of a tall building? (Be careful if you do this, and make sure an adult is with you.) It will give you a bird's-eye view of the ground below. How big are the cars, buildings, trees and roads? Do they look the same shape as they do from the ground?

Here is a bird's-eye view of some things on a table. Can you guess what they are?

(The answers are at the bottom of the page.)

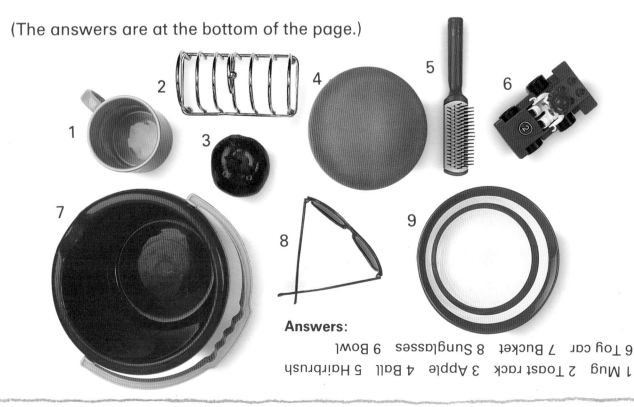

Answers:

1 Mug 2 Toast rack 3 Apple 4 Ball 5 Hairbrush 6 Toy car 7 Bucket 8 Sunglasses 9 Bowl

Maps also give you a bird's-eye view of places. They show the position of important features and leave out small details which would make the map too complicated. Maps do not show things that move about, like cars or people.

Try making a model of your street from cardboard boxes. Stand on a chair above your model street to get a bird's-eye view. Draw a map of what you see from above, showing everything in position.
Just draw the edges of the buildings, trees and shops and keep your map simple. How is your map different from the model?

A lot of modern maps are based on photographs taken from an aeroplane. These are called aerial photographs and they show a bird's-eye view of the ground.

Look carefully at this aerial photograph. Can you see the roads, houses, fields, trees and the river?
What other features can you spot?

This is a map of the area shown in the aerial photograph. It shows you the position of all the important features on the ground.

How is the map different from the photograph? Which features on the aerial photograph has the map-maker put on the map? Which features has the map-maker left out?

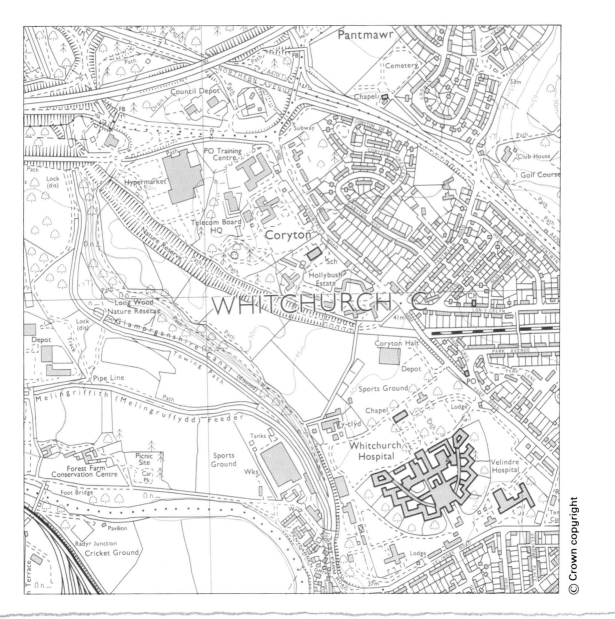

11

Talking pictures

Maps need to be simple and easy to read. There isn't room on a map to show everything in detail, so simple pictures, called symbols, are used to show the main features and landmarks. Symbols can stand for things such as churches, campsites, bridges, airports, zoos, beaches and woods.

Usually a list at the edge of the map explains what the symbols mean. This list is called a key.

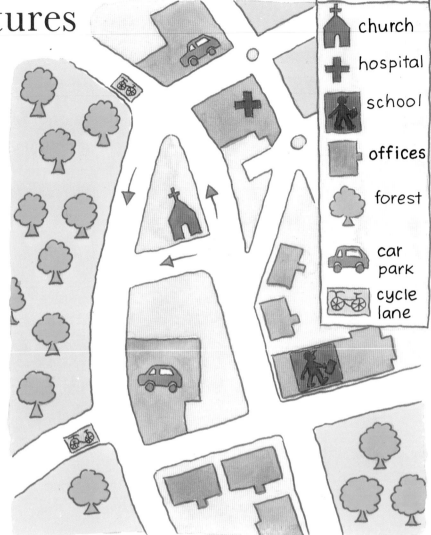

Key
- church
- hospital
- school
- offices
- forest
- car park
- cycle lane

Can you guess what these symbols might stand for?

(The answers are at the bottom of the page.)

1
2
3
4
5
6
7

Answers:

1 Post office   2 Swimming pool   3 Telephone   4 Library   5 Beach   6 Ice rink   7 Bus station

12

Imagine you are a map-maker who has to draw a map of a new farm trail opening in your local area. The map needs to show where all the different animals are. Make up symbols for all the animals and draw them on to your map. Which other places do you need to add? What about toilets, a gift shop and a cafe?

Add a key at the side of the page to explain what the symbols mean.

Ups and downs

Have you ever used a map to help you find your way on a country walk? The map is flat, so how do you know where the hills are?

One way of showing high and low ground on a map is by using imaginary lines called contour lines. Contour lines join up all the points on the map which are the same height above the sea. If the lines are close together, the land is steep. If the lines are far apart, the land is flatter.

Look carefully at these two pictures. Can you see where the hills are?

Ailsa Craig, Scotland

Inverness, Scotland

Now look at the orange contour lines on these two maps. The contour lines will show you where the land is hilly and where it is flat. Can you match up the hills and the flat land on the maps with the hills and the flat land on the pictures? Which is the map of the hilly island Ailsa Craig, and which is the map of the flat land around Inverness?

(The answers are at the bottom of the page.)

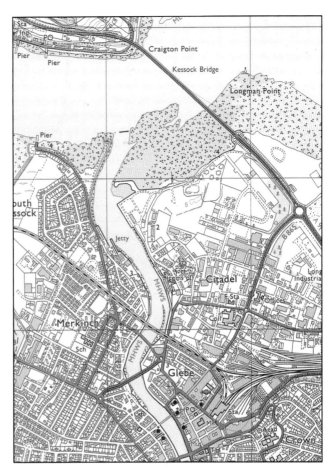

Map A

© Crown copyright

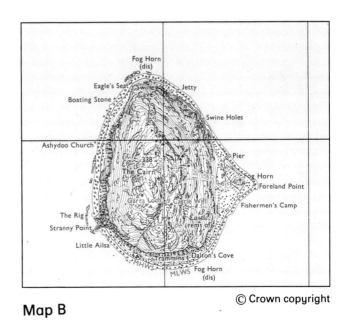

Map B

© Crown copyright

Answers:

Map B = Ailsa Craig
Map A = Inverness

How far is it?

Maps are drawn much smaller than real places. All the details of a place are measured and shrunk by the same amount. This is called drawing to scale.

Look at this map of Bee Town. The scale is marked at the bottom of the map. It tells you that one footprint on the map is equal to 5 metres on the ground. Can you work out the distance of each of these journeys?

(The answers are at the bottom of the page.)

1 From the school to the library
2 From the swimming pool to the park
3 From the bus station to the supermarket

1 = 5m

Answers:

3 40 metres
2 95 metres
1 55 metres

16

The girl in this picture is working out the distance between two places on a map. The scale on the map looks like this:

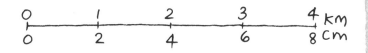

It tells her that 2cm on the map is equal to 1km on the ground.

First she traces the route between the two places with a piece of wool, making sure she follows all the bends in the roads. Next she measures the length of wool in centimetres. Then she uses the scale to work out how many centimetres on the map stand for how many kilometres in the real place.

Which way is it?

Maps usually have an arrow pointing north to help people work out which direction they are going in. South is at the bottom of the map. West is to the left and east is to the right.

Look carefully at this map of Thor. Which direction does the White Knight have to go in to reach the castle? Are the mountains to the east or west of Thor? Which direction is the dragon's lair?

N
↑

The children in the picture are finding out the direction of some landmarks in their town. They have a map of the town and a compass. A compass has a tiny magnetic needle which always points north.

First they find out where they are on the map. Then, making sure that the north on the compass is lined up with the compass needle, they turn the map around until the north arrow on the map points in the same direction as the compass needle. Then they can work out the direction of the landmarks in their town.

Finding places

Pretend you have just found this map of the planet Harg in the ruins of an old spaceship. It shows where to find the treasure hidden by the great ruler Mixos, when the planet was taken over by aliens.

The lines criss-crossing the map are called grid lines. Each line has a number or a letter. The lines divide the map into squares which can make it easier to find places quickly.

The treasure is hidden at 4H – this is called a grid reference. Find line 4 along the bottom and line H along the side. Slide one finger along line 4 and another finger along line H until they touch at point 4H.

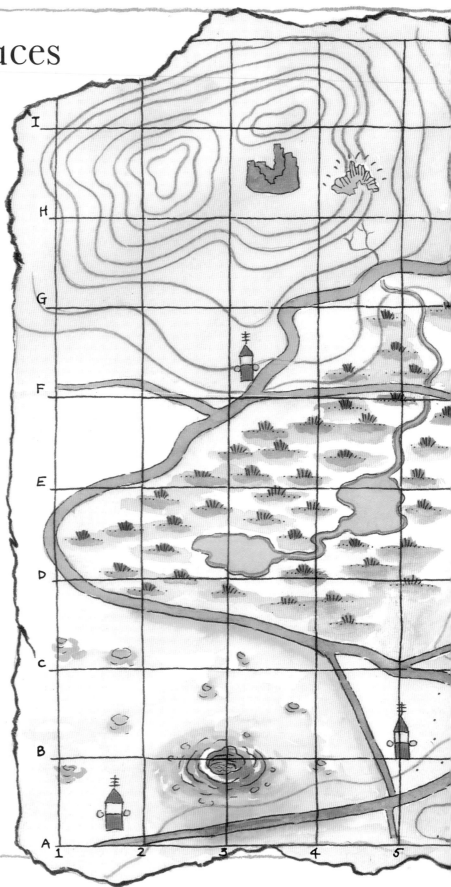

20

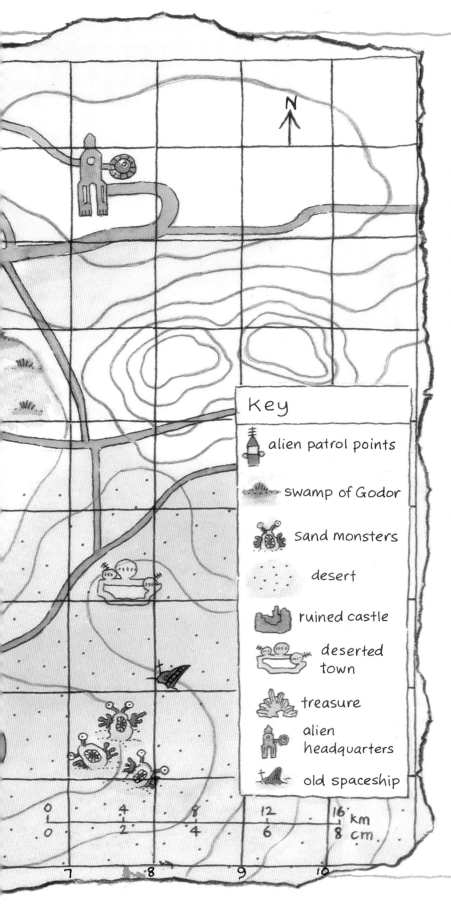

Key

🛰️ alien patrol points

🌿 swamp of Godor

👾 sand monsters

· · · desert

🏰 ruined castle

👾 deserted town

✨ treasure

🛸 alien headquarters

† old spaceship

| 0 | | 4 | | 8 | | 12 | | 16 km |
| 0 | | 2 | | 4 | | 6 | | 8 cm |

Can you plan the best route to the treasure?

Look carefully at the key. You must go round the swamp of Godor and avoid the sand monsters in the desert. You can travel by road, but you must avoid the alien patrol points.

Look at the contour lines to find the hills and the flat land.

Can you use the scale to work out how far you have to travel?

Can you find the secret store of underground water at 3B? What is the grid reference for the ruined castle?

Is the treasure hidden in the north, south, east or west?

Reading maps

When you know how to read the lines and symbols on a map, they will be able to give you a lot of information about a place.

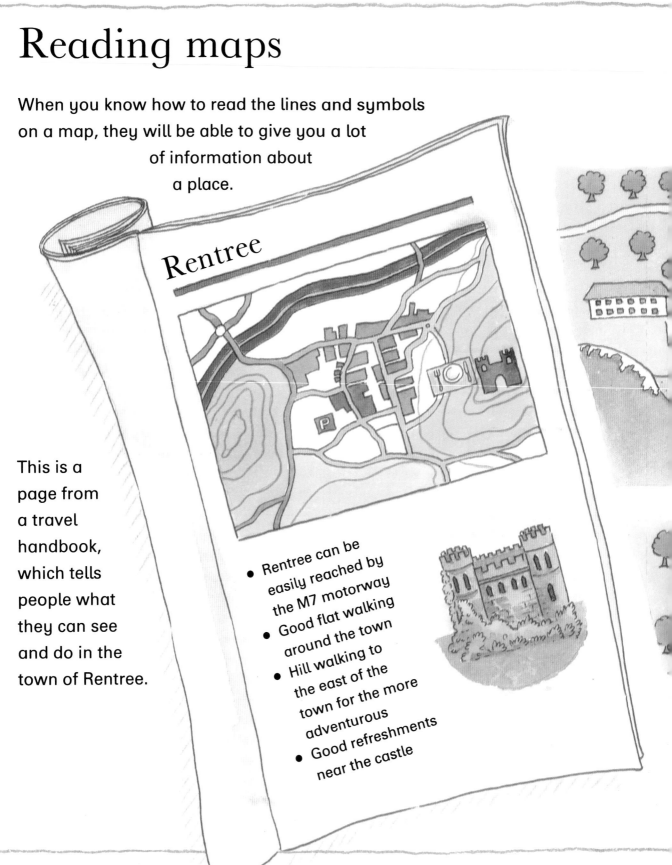

Rentree

This is a page from a travel handbook, which tells people what they can see and do in the town of Rentree.

- Rentree can be easily reached by the M7 motorway
- Good flat walking around the town
- Hill walking to the east of the town for the more adventurous
- Good refreshments near the castle

Imagine that you are writing the information for these three places. Use the map of each place to help you pick out the features. Think carefully about the information given by the signs and symbols on each map.

Cocklemouth

key
🔲 church
🏨 hotel
⛺ camp-site
🏊 swimming
🍽 restaurant
P car park
🌳 woodland

Riverside

key
🌲 woodland
🐎 pony-trekking
🥅 fishing
🛶 boat hire
🟫 buildings
⌣ bridge
〰 hills
🔲 church
P car park
- - - footpath

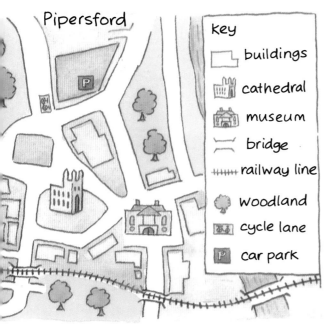

Pipersford

key
▱ buildings
🏰 cathedral
🏛 museum
⌣ bridge
+++ railway line
🌳 woodland
🚲 cycle lane
P car park

Next time you go for a walk in the countryside, see if you can follow your route on a map. Can you work out how far you walked and which direction you walked in? Were there any special features in the area to look out for?

Making maps

Try drawing some maps of your own. You might draw a map of your town or perhaps make up an imaginary map of a faraway land. Think carefully about how you're going to draw your map. Will it have grid lines to help people find places? Maybe you'll add symbols and a key to point out special features and landmarks.

My map shows the hilly countryside near my house.

I've drawn a map of my bedroom to scale.

My map's a treasure map with grid lines.

Make a ghostly grid game like this one using grid references
and compass directions to tell people what to do. Throw
dice to see how many squares to move the counters.

Old and new maps

People have been making maps for more than 4,000 years. Maps drawn a long time ago can help us to find out what people thought the world looked like.

The first maps of the whole world were drawn about 1,800 years ago. They were drawn by hand and were not very accurate, as people did not know that America, Australia and Antarctica existed. Mapmakers filled in the gaps with decorations of things like exotic animals and sea serpents.

This Anglo-Saxon world map is about 1,500 years old.

About 800 years ago, in Medieval times, maps were based on writings in the Bible. Jerusalem was always shown as the centre of the world.

A Medieval map of the world.

Nowadays, most maps are drawn by computers using satellite pictures of the Earth together with detailed measurements of the ground. These computers can draw maps to illustrate all kinds of information, such as the weather or types of farming.

HUMAN POPULATION DENSITY

1984   4.75 BILLION

NASA/GISS

0   2   4   6   8   10   30   50   70   90 200 400   1750

PEOPLE/SQ KM

The colours on this computer map show the number of people living in different parts of the world.

In the future, it may be possible to make detailed maps of other planets. Would you like to be a map-maker?

Index

For parents and teachers
More about the ideas in this book

Pages 6/7 As well as being used for finding the way, maps also record things like the weather, farming patterns, sizes of populations and the position of stars in the sky.

Pages 8/11 The key feature of a map is that it is a view seen from above. Details are added with symbols and labels. Nowadays, computers can plot maps from aerial photographs much faster than people can draw maps by hand.

Pages 12/13 Map-makers use symbols to pack a lot of information into a small space. Some symbols, such as those on tourist maps, look like the features they represent. But many symbols are graphic representations of real features.

Pages 14/15 Apart from contours, height on a map can be shown with shading, hachures (lines that follow the slope of the hills) or colours. Low ground is usually yellow or green, higher land is brown and mountain tops are purple and white.

Pages 16/17 Looking at toys as scale models of real objects may help children to understand scale on a map. A large scale map covers a small area with lots of detail. A small scale map shows a big area. The scale on a map may be written out in numbers (2cm = 1m), displayed as a representative fraction (1:50,000) or drawn as a linear scale.

Pages 18/19 Today, most maps point north, but in the past, maps have pointed south or east.

Pages 20/21 Grid references help people to find places on a map. Children could make up a game like battle ships, in which they have to locate the position of each other's ships, using grid references.

Pages 22/25 Maps are packed with information. They give clues about the shape and use of the land, the transport in an area, and the history of a place.

Pages 26/27 Encourage the children to investigate the history of map-making and to compare old maps of the whole world with modern maps made with the help of satellites and computers.

Things to do

Going places provides starting points for all kinds of cross-curricular work based on geography and the environment, looking at your locality and at the wider world.

Finding the way explores different aspects of maps and map-making, from following directions and using symbols and scale to following a route and identifying geographical features on a map.

1 Make a collection of different types of maps, using sources such as stamps, flags, T-shirts, carrier bags, travel brochures and maps of museums or hotels. What do the different maps show? How are they drawn and coloured?

2 Make a detailed map of the school, to scale, and encourage the children to take turns to direct each other to different parts of the school. The map could be given to people who visit the school. Can they find their way around successfully?

3 Find out what the local town looked like one hundred years ago and draw a map to show the position of different features. Make the map look old by stamping on it with muddy boots, spilling tea on it, rubbing sand or soil over it and scrunching it up in a ball. Many old maps were not very accurate and often used realistic pictures of hills or castles rather than symbols. The pictures took up a lot of space on the map.

4 Make up the symbols for a weather map. Decide how to show rain, snow, clouds, sunshine, thunder and lightning, fog and strong winds. It's best to keep the symbols simple, clear and easy to draw. Solid black shapes show up well if the symbols are going to be small on the map.

5 Find out more about the natural forces that have shaped our planet. Deep inside the Earth, powerful forces push up the surface of the land and pull it down. Volcanoes build up new land and earthquakes change the shape of the surface. Rain, snow, wind and ice wear away the land and carve it into new shapes. Natural landscape features have to be measured and plotted on maps.

6 Draw a flower map or a tree map of a route in the local area. Walk along a familiar road or path and mark where there are trees or flowers. Make up symbols for each kind of tree or flower and draw a key at the side of the map to show what each symbol stands for.

7 Make a simple compass using a magnet, a needle, a slice of cork and a saucer of water. Stroke the needle along the magnet about 50 times in the same direction. This will turn the needle into a magnet. Float the cork on the saucer of water and balance the needle on top. The needle will point north-south. Check the direction with a real compass and mark north and south on the edge of the saucer.

8 Draw a map to go with a favourite story or a story you have made up. Maps in a story help people to build up a picture of imaginary lands, or imagine journeys made by the characters in the story.

9 Look at a globe and see if you can find the country you live in. Globes show the sizes of countries more accurately than flat maps in atlases. Compare the size of your country on a globe with a map in an atlas. Is it the same size? Flat maps in atlases do not show the world accurately because the world is round and cannot be turned into a flat map without stretching out some areas and squashing other areas together. For instance, Mexico and Greenland are really almost the same size. But in an atlas, Grenland looks much larger than Mexico.

10 Draw a map with grid lines on the top and make up a quiz for your friends. Give them the grid references of different places on the map and see if they can tell you which place each grid reference stands for.